T0046874

ONE IMPOSSIBLE STEP

ORIDES FONTELA

ORIDES FONTELA

ONE IMPOSSIBLE STEP

SELECTED POEMS

TRANSLATED BY CHRIS DANIELS

NIGHTBOAT BOOKS
NEW YORK

© 2006 Herdeiros de Orides Fontela
© 2006 Cosac Naify
© 2006 Viveiros de Castro Editora
English translation copyright © 2023 by Chris Daniels
All rights reserved

Printed in the United States

ISBN: 978-1-643-62155-5

Design, typesetting, and author portrait by Kit Schluter
Typeset in Adobe Caslon Pro and Futura

Cataloging-in-publication data is available
from the Library of Congress

Nightboat Books
New York
www.nightboat.org

CONTENTS

from **TRANSPOSITION** (1969)

One step from my own spirit.
One impossible step from God.
Attentive to the real: here.
I happen here.

Speech

All
will be difficult to say:
the real word
is never easy.

All will be hard:
pitiless light
excessive coexistence excess
ive knowledge of being.

All will be
able to wound. Will be
aggressively real.
So real it rends us.

There is no pity in signs
nor even in love: being
is excessively lucid
and word is dense and wounds us.

(Every word is cruelty.)

Settling

O bird, in my hand
are met
your intact liberty
my acute consciousness.

O bird, in my hand
your chant
of pure vitality
meets my humanity.

O bird, settled
in my hand,
will it be possible for us
to sing in unison

if you are the rare settling
of living feeling
and I, lament spilt
into word?

Towers

To construct abstract towers
yet the struggle is real. Our vision
builded upon struggle. The real
will ache in us forever.

Skein

A braid is undone:
hands calmly
loosen threads
inutilize
the amorously woven.

A braid is undone:
hands seek the depth
of the inexhaustible net
annulling weft
and form.

A braid is undone:
hands seek the end
of time and the beginning
of themselves, before
created weft.

Hands
destroy, seeking themselves
before braid and memory.

Hands

With hands bare
to work the field:

hands wounding themselves
on beings, rough edges
of underlying unity

hands unearthing
lightfragments
of the anterior mirror.

With hands bare
to work the field:

to denude the essential star
with no pity for the blood.

Mummy

Liana
lanyard
line.

Turns and more turns
tight concentric
turns.

White spirals
white screen
unguent incense bruising
aromas.

Lianas
lanyards of expectancy
incubating sleep.

Indivisible white
line:
archaic white around
nothing.

Chart

There is an intact bearing, an
absolute aridity
in the bird that settles. In it,
settling is the chart: there is no more
need for flight.

Stone

Stone is transparent:
silence sees and seen
in its density.

(Clear texture and in
tegral definitive verb
stone silences.)

Verb is transparent:
silence contains it
in pure eternity.

Thirst

1.

To drink the hour
to drink water
to get drunk
on water alone.

2.

Water? Only this
purifies.

3.

Greater spring
unhidden spring
with neither Narcissus
nor flowers.

4.

Blessèd be thirst
for tearing our eyes away
from stone.

Blessèd be thirst
for teaching us the purity
of water.

Blessèd be thirst
for gathering us around
the spring.

Star

Over the landscape a point
of complete cosmic light
and fixed scene
that does not enclose it.

The star completes
the unity it does
not inhabit.

Challenge

Against the flowers I live
against limits
against appearance pure attention
builds a field with no more garden
than essence.

Series

First
the plea
(word parallel
to universe).

Then
powers invoked
forms plotted pure
ludic map.

Finally
act's conclusion
love to be
possible dawns
lucid.

Rose

I murdered the name
of the flower
and the very flower complex form
I simplified into symbol
(yet without eliding the blood).

But if uniquely
the word FLOWER—the word
in itself is humanity
how anymore express
non-verbal, living density?

(Ex-rose, twilight
the horizon.)

I murdered the word
and hold my living hands in blood.

Sensation

I see the bird sing
I touch this song with my nerves
its taste of honey. Its form
generating itself from the bird
as aroma.

I see the bird sing and through
denser perception
I hear distance open
like a rose
in silence.

from **HELIANTHUS** (1973)

Silver

I

Light weighing upon
        silver.
Tense   light
aches   wounds
    argent note
    offered.

Light vibrating upon
       the mirror

form   light modulating   ripe
crystal   silver glaring   fixed.

II

Silver field—shield—
       and athwart
silence unforeseen (ancient)
        and full.

Transparent waters   silence
—shield raised in silence—field
of transparency and of silver.

III

Boats came. Plains
of salt and wave coagulated
in austere silence (silver):   time
annuls in that coming.

They came
nunc et semper
living sails.

All the modes of silence (even
the most austere)   congealed in
                                                    wings
of living boats (silver)   and the non
                                                    time
is horizon   port   white
                                                    glow
of open plains . . . Field in silver.

IV

Crystal   white page
nudity?   nothing?
Field of possibles. Dawn.
And the helianthus
                         —full —
                                        over silver.

Seven Bird Poems

1.

The bird is definitive—:
we do not seek it:
it will elect us.

2.

If it were the hour of the bird
you'd open and know
the eternal moment.

3.

It will never be the same,
our atmosphere:
we uphold the flight
that holds us up.

4.

The bird is lucid
and lacerates us.
We bleed. No possible
scarring in this
direction.

5.

This bird is plumb:
it architects the real and is the very real.

6.

We'll never know
such purity:
bird devouring us
while we sing it.

7.

In light of full flight
we will exist in this bird:
it lives us.

Flight (II)

Wings of
snow
seek the
white the
perfect
peak.

Wings against
blue
mountain against blue

blue—and—white.

Earth far
below.
Far below the smell
of blood.

Poemites[1]

a) *morning*
No one yet. Roses greet me
and I greet the silence
of roses.

b) *absence*
No one here
and clouds.

c) *bird*
Wings hanging in
lightinstant.

d) *moon*
Integrality.
Fixity.

e) *Narcissus*
Flower water face
flower water
flower.

---

1. On the Mulheres de São João website, Fontela describes "Poemites" as
"Bits of my poems that I couldn't get right, so I just used the best image in
them. But some of them really were written as micro-poems. The micro-poem
is a modern tendency."

f) *spring*
From not-waiting
flowers
occur.

g) *lake*
Water's
chill
tension:
peace—in—being.

h) *waiting*
Open windows.
Door merely, slightly, ajar . . .

i) *vase*
but incommunicant.

j) *end*
Absence of roses. The way
now with no one, to silence.

Elegy (I)

But what use is the bird?
We contemplate it inert.
We touch it in its magic flash of feathers.
What use is the bird if we
possess it denatured?

What was flight is, here, now,
lethal concretion and
paralyzed color, silent, clearcut iris,
what was infinite is, here, now,
weight and form, fixed, ludic verb

what was bird and is
the object: game
of an innocence that
contemplates and revives it
—child groping
a scheme of distances
in the bird—

but what use is the bird?

The bird is no use. Arrhythmic
soft wings settle.

Impressions

Crest
of ruddy palm:
        "life."

Lake
of muddy yellow:
        "time."

Cube
of opaque metal:
        "God."

Aurora (II)

Form founds
in a single act

form's light is a unique
apex

the fruit is a unique form
fully founded

(love uniquely is
when it in-forms).

. . . but it costs the Sun to cross the desert
    but it costs the light to ripen
    but it costs the blood to sense the horizon

Genesis

An archaic bird
(with savor of
origin)
hovered (arcane bird)
over the seas.

A bird,
moving
mirroring
on high waters, unveiled
the blood.

A silent bird
opened
its
wings
—full of deep light—
over the waters.

A bird
mutely invoked
the abyss.

Ode

And while we bite
live fruits
evening declines.

And while we fix
clear signs
silence flows.

And while we suffer
the intense hour

slowly time
wastes us.

from **ALBA** (1983)

One step
from the bird
I breathe
in.

The Trades

Fruit for
      acid
sun for
      secret
ocean for
      nucleus

space for
      escape
escape for
      silence

—wealth for
      nakedness.

Mosaic

Strong erect angels.

Neutral
faces
luminous
raiment
quiet
immobile
wings.

Angels.
Unremovable.

Map

Here is the chart of the skies:
live distances
indicate only
itineraries
the stars do not interconnect
and the greatest distance
is merely looking.

Star
only flight and light
always born now:
she does not recognize her sisters
and has no mirror.

Here is the chart of the skies: all
indeterminate and unforeseen
creates a fluent love
forever alive.

Here is the chart of the skies: every

                              thing

                                    moves.

Cycle (II)

Birds
return
always and
always.

Time fulfills itself. Evanescent
form built
being
and
rhythm.

Birds
return. Always
birds.

Childhood returns very slowly.

Poem

To know silence by heart
diamond and/or mirror
the silence beyond
white.

To know its weight
its sign
—to inhabit its im
    placable
    star.

To know its center: empty
splendor beyond
life
and life beyond
memory.

To know silence by heart

—and profane it, dissolve it
                  in words.

Vigil

Absolute
      moment:
living bird
attentive to.

Tense in the
        instant
—immobile flight—
full presence
bird and
    sign

(white open
and vivid
      attention).

Immobile bird.
Living bird
attentive
to.

Ode (II)

Surprise-instant: birds
traversing silence

surprise
instant: enameled
immobile shells

the instant
this quiet stone.

from **ROSACE** (1986)

Things swept together
into hazard
mixed
—most beautiful universe.

—HERACLITUS

Initiation

If you come to a strange land
bow down

if this place is outlandish
bow down

if the day is all strangeness
submit

—you are infinitely more strange.

Nocturne

Those born of night
who, among bones, watch
                    over the fire
those who watch the stars
and, oppressed, breathe
                    in caves

those who will live despite
darkness and light
burning clandestine
                    in their eyes

those who do not dream, those nightborn
did not come to play: her breast
guards a single word.

Aristocrat

The savage will not
learn
the savage will not
turn
the savage will not
bow down

(mythological savage.)

Pyramid

There it is
pain of thousands   our
anonymous strength

(from pharaoh
not a cinder.)

Garden

Cool shadows
lean
over waters

springs
      spurt   stones
                  hush

shine of
flowers:
      burnt sweetness.

                  Thirst so
                  acid
                  and water
                  so brief.

                  * * *

                  Bird so instant
                  aneous: not even
                  its flight is caught
                  by the waters.

Birds
come
devour
fruits
peck at
living
grains

swift
they part
(dream of
birds)

eternal
aerial
free.

I sow suns
and sounds
in living earth

sink my
feet
in the ground: sow
and go.

Harvest doesn't matter.

Legend

In the blind root of this wonder
there is a crystal: whomsoever stares upon it

ah, whomsoever stares upon it
eyes in blood
hands in blood
living blood

whomsoever stares upon it will not sleep
but will be a crystal of wonder

—will remain lucid forever.

Ode

In this all
all is missing

(mist)

and in this
missing:
everything.

Sphinx

There are no questions.
Obdurate silence grows wild.

from **WEB** (1996)

Lucidity
maddens

To See

To see
the back
of the sun the
womb
of chaos the
bones.

To see. To see one's self.
To say nothing.

Speech

I speak of woodland
birds   of suns
     unquenched
     of rooted
     stones

of living
blood   of stars
unceasing.

I speak of what holds
back sleep.

Exemplars

Plato
fixing forms

Heraclitus
worshiping fire

Socrates
loyal to his Daemon.

Cocoon

Cocoon:
hidden

work
sleep's
work.

Silk:
work

future
butterfly.

Sleep:
work

meta
morphosis's
acute weft.

Dove

Coos lust
disturbed
        skies
gray
wings
ash Aphrodite
bird!

(love
exact blindness).

Narcissus (Games)

Everything
happens in the
mirror.

* * *

Spring
empties into very
spring.

* * *

I read
my hand:
my only
book.

* * *

A god
I eye
eye
to
eye.

* * *

Life has us: we have nothing
                                                        else.
Light is
            in us: we illumine.

* * *

The adventure
—the
      venture—
to flow
forever.

* * *

Never to love
what does not
vibrate

never to believe
in what does not
sing.

* * *

We see by mirror
and riddle

(but would there be another
way to see?

* * *

The mirror dissolves
time

the mirror deepens
the riddle

the mirror devours
the face.

The Anti-Bird

A bird
its nest is stone

its cry
gray metal

aches in the space
of its eye.

A bird
weighs
and hunts
amid garbage
amid boredom.

A bird
resists the
skies. And endures.
Despite.

Night

To hide (to forget)
the face

to inter (to occult)
the light

to darken
love to
sleep.

To watch over what is born.

Lullaby

To hear a
bird
is it now or
never

is it childhood
or pure
moment?

To hear a
bird
is
always

(it aches deep in
thought).

Angel

I

An angel
is fire:
it is consumed.

An angel
is gaze:
it introverts.

II

An angel
is crystal:
it dissolves.

An angel
is light
and goes out.

Door

The stranger
knocks:
from inner amplitude
there is no reply.

It is the stranger (the brother) who knocks
but there will never be
a reply:

welcome's country
is far to go.

Vesper

The evening star is
ripe
and without any perfume.

The evening star is
barren
and most high:

after her is
only silence.

POETICS

On Poetry and Philosophy—A Testimony[2]

Being is high agony, a difficult ordeal:
is to surpass among metamorphoses
and—living essence in supreme purity—
to strip sorceries, mists, myths.

That root is high agony, purity
of extreme contingency given drink
at the seas of full Being and, enraptured,
made sole in its lucid fruit.

Being is high agony: essential
human toil and superhuman grace
of our rebirth in utter solitude

and in solitude—pain borne and glory—
in our contingency we bear
the essential weight of deep love.

This sonnet, which I wrote when I was 23, is crucial for me: it is a kind of program for my life. I have never reneged upon it; I will never be able to fulfill it; yet, it is my task to try. "A difficult ordeal," yes, in fact impossible; this properly constitutes the human. And, of course, all tools are useful, mainly religion (the

2.   In the original text, OF does not include the entire sonnet which opens the essay. She merely quotes the first line. I added the full poem and have altered the first two sentences of the essay. The sonnet is dated "10.25.63," and appears toward the end of *Rosace*.

mystical side of it), poetry—basic and musical intuitions, which I was born with—and a much more recent tool, philosophy. Leaving religion aside (but it remains, deep down), I'll speak only of poetry and philosophy.

Poetry is archaic as the word, old as the canticle. Poetry, like myth, also thinks and interprets being, but it is not pure, lucid thought. Poetry welcomes the irrational, the dream, invents and opens fields of reality. Poetry sings. It can be lucid, if one is able to think—it is a logos—but it is not restricted to that. It doesn't matter: poetry is neither madness nor fiction, but rather a highly useful tool for grasping the real—or at least that is my ideal of poetry. Then comes the struggle for objectivity and lucidity, philosophy. Fruit of human maturity, philosophy slowly emerges out of poetry and myth, and still bears the marks of co-birth, the living traces of poetic intuition. For no one has ever managed to be one hundred percent lucid and objective; this has never happened. It would be inhuman; it would be madness and barrenness. Well, there we already have a basic difference between poetry and philosophy—the age, the technique, not the scope. For the purpose of understanding the real is always the same, it is "high agony" and through "a difficult ordeal" we must try to realize our humanity. This is what I have to say, initially, about philosophy and poetry.

Well, I've always done poetry, and I've always been curious. "What animal is that?" was my student question. "Ti esti," "what is it?," asks the philosopher. It's the same question... At sixteen I wrote the following lines:

> Thinking hurts
> and gets you nowhere.

Bad lines, valid intuition. Thinking really can hurt, can tickle, can be as irrepressible as the student's curiosity. And what's the use? Well, the thing is, I've never bought readymade answers, I've always wanted to go there myself, to try, to test. I tried through poetry. Now, a basic intuition of my poetry is "to be here"—self-discovery and discovery of everything, problematizing everything at the same time. But this "to be here" is also to be "one step from"—from my spirit, from the bird, from God—and this one step is the "impossible" with which I struggle. It is the paradox I express in a poem:

NEAR STAR

Near: but still
star
— much more star
than near.

Now, the basic existential position of my poems is already philosophical, that is, it would be possible to develop it philosophically; hence my interest in philosophy itself. I lived the almost ineffable intuition of being just "one step from." I felt that it would be enough to lift a single veil. Ah, youth! And then explicit philosophy comes into my life. I took classes at the Escola Normal, read the books I managed to get ahold of (Pascal, Gilson, Maritain, and even some not so orthodox), and mixed in my interest in mysticism—Huxley, Saint Tereza, Saint John of the Cross. The mishmash resulted in my book *Transposition*, which is very "abstract" and "thought"—in the

83

poetic sense of such terms. It revolved around the problem of being and lucidity, and abused the term "light." A strange book; recently I realized it went against the grain of Brazilian poetry, which is generally sensual and sentimental. It even looked something like João Cabral de Melo Neto, due to its analytical turn, but it never was, of course. It was a book written in the countryside, informed by my own interests; poetry and philosophy were already trying to merge, as much as possible.

I don't need to explain because my interest in philosophy was almost innate, like poetry was. So, I jumped at the opportunity to actually do philosophy. Maybe it would have turned into something practical (it didn't), but what interested me was, believe it or not, the Truth. Was this naivety? Today I know it was, but it was the very noble ingenuousness without which one cannot believe. I went on with philosophy, continuing with poetry, naturally. And the curious thing is that these waters did not mix any further. If they had, my poetry would have become dry and unspontaneous. But I was lucky (!) not to become a philosopher . . . In fact, the most I could have done was to become a professor of philosophy, that is, a technician in the subject—and, well, that was not the purpose. It couldn't be; I lacked the economic and cultural base. I was poor and coming only from Escola Normal all I could do was finish the course. But I had a lot of fun.

No, I concluded, philosophy itself is not exactly my path; in fact, I don't even consider myself an intellectual. I'm a poet, period. Better to create than comment, of course. Philosophy didn't give me the answer. Poetry only gives insights; the near star keeps moving farther and farther away, but one keeps on writing . . .

If I became dissatisfied with philosophy itself, that doesn't mean it was useless. It gave me a cultural base I didn't have; it enlarged my world. And it gave me the "status" of "philosopher," university student. It's more or less myth, but myths are excellent for promoting books.

Poetry went on. I was concerned with form, technique—*Helianthus*, from my college days—and even achieved meta-poetry—*Alba*. Then I tried to go back, make the conversation more concrete—*Rosace*, *Web*. Closer to everyday life, more deeply and at times painfully lived, is how it is now, and so am I. Consequences of poverty, aging, sorrows. I'm sorry to have lost my past ingenuousness (and immunity) but I haven't changed my skin, that's impossible. The future is properly speaking the unpredictable—and I don't know where poetic research and my untrammeled thinking will take me. And I've also added Zen Buddhism to my mishmash—with good results, by the way—and now I'm looking for other "ingredients," if possible. Not being satisfied is very human.

The sonnet I referred to at the beginning speaks of

strip[ping] sorceries, mists, myths

and that's a very philosophical task, if philosophy were only critical awareness and lucidity, if it didn't also feed mists and myths of its own. Without which we would be so naked that we would die, or who knows—maybe we transmute ourselves. I chase

meta

morphosis's

acute weft[3]

---

3. See "Cocoon," pg. 68.

and, for that, poetry, philosophy, Zen and whatever else comes along, everything works on the way to the unsaid, the never-said, the inexpressible.

In another poem, I say:

love
exact blindness[4]

If we understand "love" as the primordial creative energy, then poetic knowledge takes place as an "exact blindness": intuition, untamed thought. Poetry, of course, contains no proof: this is a task for philosophy. But philosophers—the really creative ones—also start from intuitions, and it is poetry that gives us something to think about. Think of the exhilarating fragments of Heraclitus. Religious mystery . . . Philosophy? Poetry? Same thing! And Plato, also a poet? What about Heidegger—who I confess to having read as poetry—who ends up in the poetic, after trying so hard to say something unsayable? There is a lot of poetry in philosophy. Not didactic poetry, like the pre-Socratics—but poetry as a source that inspires and intoxicates. And I've spoken of philosophy in poetry, but it is a "philosophy" that is not known, that sings—that gives a poem its nerves and tries to go where reason cannot.

Philosophers can serve as an example to poets, as I say:

Socrates
loyal to his Daemon[5]

---

4.   See "Dove," pg. 69.
5.   See "Exemplars," pg. 67.

86

On the Way to Clover

> "I was, like the weeds, and no one pulled me out."
> —FERNANDO PESSOA / ÀLVARO DE CAMPOS

PREHISTORY: First literary influence? My father, illiterate and all. But every night he told me a fairy tale. The plot of these tales was basically the same, but the adventures were always new. I remember one in which the hero, who lived in modern times, entered a mythical realm and . . . installed electricity! Amazing. It seemed like my father still lived in Middle Ages and dreamed of inventing the perpetual motion machine. By such logic I should be looking to square the circle; it's just that I'm looking for the "circulation of the square." But I'm not so much different from my father.

. . . My mom? She taught me how to read and write—ABCs and ear-pulling. And, in the primer, I found poems, like the national anthem. Should I also mention, as prehistory, Rádio Nacional and "folk" poems? Well, that's enough about prehistory: it was the Stone Age!

FOLKLORE: By which I mean the time of my first ingenuous little poems in the children's newspaper and even—whoa!—a poem recited at the pulpit (it was for Our Lady). But since this is all pretty silly stuff, I'll start talking about my pre-literary phase, so to speak.

SCHOOL: I got in (I was very lucky). I wrote my first sonnets, learned metrics with my late teacher Francisco Pascoal and with

Gonçalves Dias ("A Tempestade"). I read, at that time, Manuel Bandeira and Alphonsus de Guimaraens, and all the minors, etc. For better or worse, I acquired the aura of a municipal poet and for the local taste I was great. Since I was 16, I have had poems published in the city's newspapers (mainly, or exclusively, *O Município*). All very local, Tree Day, Mother's Day, Christmas. If I'd stayed on that, I'd still be there, and that would be fine. How did I change and manage to achieve, if not great literature, at least something, let's say, state level, something that São Paulo residents would accept? That's the first real problem, and it's a little mysterious, even to me . . .

EDUCATION: Strange years, from 16 to 25, more or less. I read and discovered Carlos Drummond de Andrade, the main influence in my life. I also discovered Pessoa (introduced by my cousin), Cabral, Alfonsus de Guimaraens Filho and even Cassiano Ricardo, a dilutor emeritus, but excellent for learning technical tricks. I discovered a cousin, Ana Maria Lopes Salomão. So, there was already a group—two poets who read each other. And there were naïve attempts at contests (I tried twice, when I was 17 and 21 years old). In prose, I discovered the world: Guimarães Rosa.

Besides my cousin, I was helped at the time by Mr. Oliveira Neto (who lent me books from what I believe was the best private library in São João da Boa Vista), and the Sociedade de Cultura Artística. I was a member. I recited my poems at gatherings. And there was Madalena de Oliveira, who lent me the Literary Supplement of the *Estado de São Paulo*. I didn't have a penny, not even for a newspaper! Well, as "paideia,"[6] that was beyond derisory. But there was the laudable "hybris" of youth, which allows us—with impunity—to consider ourselves geniuses or whatever. And there was the "wild" writing, without criticism or restraint, walking alone. I had no idea where to. I don't even know now and, being admittedly a poet of inspiration, I depend on the subconscious and have never answered a crucial question: who writes? I take on a poem, rework it (when necessary), and I sign it, as this is a social necessity. But what is the origin? I had a "theory"... a daydream. Poetry was a young woman in an enchanted garden, and it was her servant who wrote and "sent," I don't know how, poems to poets. This is neither better nor worse than a lot of talk out there ... But that was the "wild" proliferation in motion: the good, the average, the horrible. Burnt notebooks. Fortunately. For the sake of curiosity, I'll quote the worst lines I can remember writing, in a horrible poem: "The Dead Virgin."

> The virgin died. Did she die of her heart or from waiting?
> And blood, blood everywhere ...

Finally, a last notable influence, notable in the sense of really formative. I have to mention a psychiatrist, Dr. Helinho, who I attended, in 1961, in Itapira. He tried to decipher all my symbols. As he couldn't really do it, it was necessary to complicate things. His diagnosis was "hypertrophy of symbology." Exactly. It was just what I needed to move from the naïve and

---

6. *Paideia* refers to the education of the ideal citizen of Ancient Greek city-states. In Ancient Rome, it was called *humanitas*.

confessional to something more elaborate. And my unconscious did that; I progressed with a few false starts here and there. The main thing was to escape from the confessional, the first person, everything that might reek—even from a distance—of "feminine poetry." I was already a feminist and knew that my poetry would be devalued if it looked like "women's poetry." So, I abstracted, abstracted, abstracted. It was a, impulse: I followed. But it was also a trap, because that's how I fell into hyper-sublimated poetry, which seemed so typical of women. I've tried to save myself from that in the last few books, and I'm still trying. But those who criticize me for being Byzantine, Hermetic, and other silly things, should know my origins, should know that I recognize my defects and limitations, and I like—I even love!—dealing with the sociology of literature. No wonder: the best case study I know is me.

PASSAGE: At 16, when I discovered myself—it was a new light, the Cogito, the Sun, the Morning Star—until my Catholic times, the reading of neo-Thomists, from which comes my interest in being, and my decision to study philosophy, I wrote and wrote and one day... I discovered that, for some time, I was no longer understood by the municipality. What had happened? Who and what influenced me? I forgot to mention Vilém Flusser (*Language and Reality*). Nonsense or not, what a wonder! From this random and self-taught diet, from these intuitions and experiences, "something" was born. All I had to do was recognize, select, take it on.

DAVI AND *ROSACE*: Professor Davi Arrigucci Jr. appeared, praising my poem "Elegia," which had come out in *Município*. With his encouragement, I prepared the book *Rosace* (which was not published). And I already had a plan: to be a professor in São Paulo, to study Philosophy at USP, to publish a book. I get it all, but in 1969, I publish not *Rosace*, but *Transposition*. (I thought it was a better book). But *Rosace* deserves analysis, despite being dead (at the time) and dissected. Its fivefold structure—speech, play, struggle, being, sharing—foreshadowed everything else, and already contained all the themes of my personal mythology—being, silence, words, poetry, blood . . . The sharing part has not developed, of course: so-called social poetry is not a subject for authentic proletarians like me. It is fine for the bourgeois to write about the poor, but if you're poor, you want to avoid the topic, the sooner the better. But time passed and I brought two books to São Paulo: *Rosace* (ready to go) and *Transposition*.

TRANSPOSITION[7]: I should hold back a bit, stop playing around. I'd already reached literary reality: what was published exists. Whether I like it or not. And I do! This book, still with a naive and very Sanjoanense flavor, with its own integrity and strength, is the child of the São João Sun! Don't look for "philosophy" in it, or Orientalism, it's just what it is, the almost ineffable intuition of being "one step from." From what? I have no idea, today I'm "light years from"... The sun became the Near Star. It is a clear and naive book, at heart, despite its excessively abstract language. It seems "theoretical," but it's fully lived. And it was *Transposition*

---

7. *Transposição*. Instituto de Cultura Hispânica da USP, São Paulo, 1969.

that I published, in 1969, via the Instituto de Espanhol at the University of São Paulo, where Davi Arrigucci worked. But before moving on to *Helianthus*, a sophisticated production by a Philosophy student at USP—because a "little teacher" has no status and would be invisible—I want to make it clear that, in all my books, nothingness has never interested me. How could it interest anyone? The problem has always been being, form, word. Silence only comes into it due to the inevitable impasse. And so up to *Alba*, because afterwards even I got tired of this subject.

HELIANTHUS[8]: Helios and anthos, Sun and flower, earth and blood, totality, circularity. I recognize that this is my most "Byzantine" book. In a good and bad sense. I used and abused all the technique I'd learned. Yes, I read the *concretistas*, but . . . it was too late. The spine was ready and erect, and other influences could only graze by me. I read Mallarmé, Baudelaire, Góngora. And very little penetrated, I was what I already was. That's why I'm not and never could be a renovator and, at most, I acquired mastery and my own way of dealing with what I received from my social environment. *Helianthus* shows as much mastery as limitation, but I believe that, at the time, its preoccupation with metapoetry (form, word) was not so out of phase. But despite Antonio Candido's sponsorship, the book was totally ignored. Bad luck . . . Now I've changed again, from a poet read only at USP to a poet known at least in some other states. This took time. Ten years, from *Helianthus* to *Alba*.

---

8.   *Helianto*. Roswitha Kempf Editores, São Paulo, 1973.

ALBA[9]: I had met Professor Antonio Candido around '70 or '71, after *Transposition*, which he liked. He read *Helianthus* and got it published, and he also read *Alba*—he ended up writing a preface for it. Was it easy? No way! It was really difficult to publish poetry at that time. But, in '83, Roswitha Kempf took over and the book was critically successful, got an award and even sold. Was I happy? Well, sure . . . For me, it was the end of a line, the apex of the poetic spiral that began, I believe, with the unpublished *Rosace I*. It was something perfect and therefore outdated and dead. They could praise or decry, but my problem was—how to change?

The previous success led to the publication of what would be the next book: *Rosace* (as exists now). As a matter of fact, before I forget, poems from *Rosace I* (the foundling) are scattered throughout all my later books. The oldest is "Composition," in *Helianthus*, which I wrote when I was 19. Well, chronology is not my exactly my forte: I group poems however I want, to compose the entirety of a book, to make sure there's an internal structure, head and feet. Chronology does come into it, of course, to some extent.

Returning to *Alba*, at this point I really had a book, something quite complete, and, for all that . . . terminal. I came back to "one step from" . . . but I'm trying to get out of it. The only novelty that I see in Alba is the beginning of the influence of Zen. Just a "smell," something subtle, noticeable in certain poems. I won't say which ones. Read the book, dammit!

---

9. *Alba*. Roswitha Kempf Editores, São Paulo, 1983.

ROSACE[10]: *Alba*'s success may have harmed *Rosace*'s structure a little, as I organized the book too quickly, and the material was very heterogeneous. New stuff, back of the drawer, scraps of memory. I put it all together. I took advantage of the aborted book's title and the five-fold structure—I owe to Davi the idea of how to organize the book—but, even so, it's kind of dissonant. I justified myself by using a koan by Heraclitus as an epigraph, that is, if the universe is an organized mess, a "chaosmos," my book could also be the same thing, tranquilly . . .

It was in *Rosace* that I tried to renew myself. I abandoned the sublime (which, as a good proletarian, I mistrust—a whole lot!), took on the personal and the concrete, that is, condensing the abstractions and presenting them as images, if possible exemplary—something along the lines of Brecht. Partly I succeeded, partly not. Anyway, I'm on my way, on a new turn, the most problematic of all.

I should point out that *Rosace* includes a Zen book—Zen in my way—and sonnets ("Bucolics") that weren't even in *Rosace I*—this was pure archeology. Also, poems that stayed in my memory . . . Are there still lost poems from *Rosace I*? Are they worth it? I don't think so. I used what survived and that was that.

CLOVER (1969-1988)[11]: A four-leaf clover. For luck. That's all for now. But our times are terrible, we are "poets in times of trouble," as Heidegger says. Our culture is in a crisis that reaches its very foundations—we call it postmodernism—because

---

10. *Rosácea*. Roswitha Kempf Editores, São Paulo, 1983.
11. *Trevo*. Duas Cidades, São Paulo, 1988.

there's not even a name for what has died and/or is yet to be born. Where am I? Where is my work of more than twenty years in the framework of Brazilian poetry? I don't know. Let friends, critics, other poets help me answer this question. I'll end this personal testimony of a writer if not exceptional, then reasonable and conscientious. In *Rosace I*, I had an epigraph from Ecclesiastes: "That which is far off and / exceeding deep, / who can find it out?" Can we? Well, the humble and even vulgar weed of poetry wasn't uprooted by anyone; it was well cultivated and turned out to be what it made: this *Clover*. And as it's all there is for now, I prefer to go back to Ecclesiastes: "Vanity of vanities, all is vanity." Or if you like, all is poetry, right?

* * *

WEB[12]: They say it's an easier book than the previous ones. But that was my intention, I wanted to get away from the Baroque. They complain, because I don't write love poems. I guess they never read Homer. [. . .] I wanted to get to the heart of things. I've already done two readings for a young audience, and they really enjoyed it. It comforts me. But unfortunately, our experts still have a very Olympian view of poetry. Before *Web*, I came to be classified as a "metaphysical poet." Now, I hope it gets harder to label me. [. . .] But it's the same old story: it's better if they talk badly, but still talk about me. I need money to live. My life is a picture of the life of retired people in Brazil. And the life of poets in the country. [. . .] I wanted to be leaner, I wanted to write exemplary poems in the fashion of Brecht. I know they

---

12. *Teia*. Geração Editorial, São Paulo, 1996.

don't like it because the fashion today is baroque. [...] Difficulty is in fashion. It's a sociological phenomenon, and it's useless to argue with the facts of sociology. [...] I don't want to go against anyone, I just want to write my poems. This little poet war is a lot of fun, but I want no part of it. I'm a poor woman, a little woman who writes good poetry, but, poor thing, she's not part of the milieu. I don't have a family, I don't own any property, I don't go to fancy places. It's like I'm storming Olympus.

—EXCERPTED FROM
"ORIDES FONTELA RESISTE À SOFISTICAÇÃO DE POESIA,"
INTERVIEW BY JOSÉ CASTELLO,
ESTADÃO, JUNE 1, 1996.

EXTRACTS FROM INTERVIEWS

from INTERVIEW OF THE MONTH

AUGUSTO MASSI, JOSÉ MARIA CANÇADO & FLÁVIO QUINTILIANO

Your first critic was Nogueira Moutinho, right?

Yeah, he wrote about *Transposition*. He was the only one who saw my first book, no one else did. When *Helianthus* was ready, I got a letter from José Paulo Paes. I no longer have this letter because of the fire where my things were lost.

When did the fire happen?

In 1981. I lost everything I had except the clothes on my back and a little money in the bank. At least I had that. And my work.

Orides, we often realize that poetry for you is not exactly a respite.

No, it's not! It's my life, I don't have anything else but poetry.

You never instrumentalize poetry or instrumentalize yourself to make poetry. Every gesture, every word has a strong poetic dimension. Is the poet's way of life wild in you?

What do you mean, "wild"?

Is it a wild way of life, being a poet?

Oh, I don't know. If by "wild" you mean on your own, without caring for anyone's opinion, going on alone . . . I wrote thousands of poems that were never published. Those that were . . . well, it's a pittance. The other originals, thank God, were burned, see, Augusto? These are things I didn't want anyone to resurrect. And they won't be resurrected, because they're destroyed. I'm "wild" in the sense of "alone." I only wasn't wild about one thing: before I published my first four books, friends read them and approved. And they were good critics, my friends. To this day I've never published anything without severe criticism from friends.

I meant "wild" in the sense of Clarice Lispector, *Close to the Wild Heart*.

I am the wild heart itself.

You are? Could you talk a little more about this?

The wild is the wild, that's all. I was poor and I was a woman. I had no one and I have nothing now. I don't have any property, even my home is in trouble. Poetry has occupied all the spaces in my life, because I don't have anything else in its place. I could never have a life of the emotions. A working-class woman, poor, in this Brazil, it's impossible. I had two choices: either the freedom to write poetry, lead my life "wildly," on my own, or what? My children would be cheap labor, they would be poor people, it wouldn't do any good. I had to choose the lesser evil. The lesser possible evil is being poor and alone. And the greatest possible good has always been poetry.

In this sense, you were aware of your choice when you came from São João . . .

My path could not be easy. For poor women it was never easy. I've been a feminist since my teens. Since the day my father said: "When you marry, you will obey your husband," and I said "No way am I gonna get married."

In that too you were wild.

Totally. And I want to die without obeying anyone. I needed to have a profession, so I became a teacher. But I never had the patience to put up with my students.

Are you retired?

No, I was "readapted." I don't know if it's better or worse than retiring. Maybe it's worse. But worse than that was putting up with other people's children, teaching others, and earning this pittance that I earn. Currently, it doesn't even give 100,000[13] a month.

[. . .]

Do you follow women poets?

---

13. Brazilian currency in 1989 was the *cruzado novo*, which was replaced by the *cruzeiro* in 1990. In the late 1980s, the Brazilian economy was in very bad shape. The currency was changed in order to fight runaway inflation. 100,000 *cruzados novos* was not enough to live on.

Well, I'm glad you asked that question. When I was young, I decided to be a feminist and realized that if I wrote sentimental, weepy, "feminine" poetry, it would devalue me. I made a thoughtful, purposeful effort to make a dry, serious, depersonalized poetry, which would at no point express my condition of being a woman. Poetry is sexless, just like mathematics is sexless, philosophy is sexless. Poetry is what it is. If I don't talk about love affairs in my poems, I can justify myself like Drummond: "I need to write a poem about Bahia, / but I never went there." I never loved anyone. I won't write about something I haven't experienced; that would be intellectual dishonesty. I speak of what I know and what I lived.

[. . .]

What you said was a little shocking: that you never wrote about love because you didn't live it. But love is one of the consecrated themes in poetry . . .

In the poetry of men, maybe. Men write about women. I don't have a "muso" to inspire me. Do you want the job? [*Laughs*]. I don't much like the language of love, like what Adélia Prado does. My experiences with love were so bad, so boring, that it's better to bury them. You can put this in the interview: I insist that we do not leave anyone the legacy of our wretchedness. If I'd gotten married, I would have had children. So, it's for the best I didn't.

from INTERVIEW WITH ORIDES FONTELA

MICHEL RIAUDEL

What affiliation would you give to your poetry?

It seems that somehow I started writing against the grain. Instead of making the more typical sensual Brazilian poetry, I did something more concrete. I didn't realize that I had already started against the grain, with a more meditative, more reasoning poetry. It was really different. And I didn't realize it. That came much later.

Well, João Cabral de Melo Neto...

Yeah. But he writes about social issues a lot, the Northeast. He has a domain all his own. I wish it rained more on his land. It's kind of dry, a little too dry, for me. The Northeast is dry, João Cabral is dry. But I wouldn't mind being an ambassador like he was, wow!

Don't you think your poetry has a little to do, not with this dry side, but with the rational side?

When I started writing, I hadn't read João Cabral de Melo Neto, I read him much later. One time, I had a fight with a philosophy professor who said I was imitating João Cabral. [*Laughter*]. I didn't imitate anything. I had written my things on my own and had read a tiny bit of João Cabral. I went nuts. The fact that I'm kind of analytical doesn't mean . . . there are coincidences, right?

$$[\ldots]$$

From the beginning, you wrote very meditative poetry, as you've said.

At least I used to. Now I'm trying to get out of it. Trying to come up with something more concrete, right? I got a little tired of it because my poetry was "contrabassing" about nothing, up in the clouds. I want something more concrete. I mean, I'm trying to change my style. That style, up in the clouds, was good until *Alba*. We get tired of subjects, like we get tired of life, of things, right?

I'm pretty confused. I don't know the right way to go. I don't know what path Brazilian poetry is on, either. I think it's at a dead end, at the end of the century. Nothing we do is new. It even feels like the experiments have all been done, the experiments were all so crazy, that . . . what are you going to do that's new? Write what you know as best as possible, that's all you can do. I already have a formed personality and changing a lot can ruin everything, it's not possible either. At 55 years old, changing everything like that, you can't.

What do you mean when you talk about more concrete poetry?

An idea expressed in a very concrete image. That's not an easy thing to do.

Do you mean that the idea passes through an image?

Exactly, more imagery. I'm not doing it very well. I don't know, I'm mixing it up. What comes up now, comes up. I don't care anymore, whatever God wants.

Does that mean you cared before?

Perhaps yes. Now I'm really confused about everything, I'm confused about life. I'm in such a big crisis, depressed, with financial problems and everything. At the moment, I don't really care about literature. It's a little secondary. All these little glories don't give me money. Look, there's someone in Rio Grande do Sul who is doing a thesis on my work, can you believe it? So, I'm in such a mess materially that intellectually I'm a little behind. Besides, there's no money even to buy books. I've been stealing a few, but buying . . . [*Laughs*]

Poetry books?

Yeah. This one, for example [*shows a Brazilian translation of Valéry's* Variété]. Though I don't like Mr. Valery very much, I really don't. I know "Le Cimetière Marin." I have a bilingual edition. The book is very beautiful, but I like the illustrations and drawings better. He's the neo-Symbolist type who knots things up an awful lot. Aristocratic to the absurd! I'm always in an incredible contradiction. A person who was never aristocratic in all my life, a real proletarian background, and my poetry is aristocratic. Well, at the beginning it was, anyway. Something like that, up there in the sky. In fact, the relationship between art and life is such an imaginary thing. Sometimes there's no way. Yeah, a proletarian background and life . . . What can I do? I was born this way. I don't even know how it happened.

[. . .]

Is your abstraction a kind of self-protection?

I don't like confessionalism at all . . . A psychiatrist I consulted when I was young tried to decipher everything I wrote. I tried to avoid that; I didn't want to be deciphered so easily [*Laughs*]. I'm not someone to be seen so easily. I'm not confessional. By the way, who's interested in confession? Nobody should be all that interested in our private lives. Not mine, not anyone's.

[. . .]

Your poetry is amazing in its ability to crystallize an image, an idea, in a few words.

A fast, low kick. That's why I liked Drummond. It's something closed, a strong, defined image. I like that. Instead of wasting a lot of words; when I'm lucky, I get it right. I like that. A really quick little poem that works right away, you get it. It starts . . . I don't have the breath for long poems, you've already noticed. I never tried a long poem. And when something of mine is a little longer, it's usually variations on a single theme. I wouldn't write a "Cimetière Marin" like Valery. Maybe I'm incapable of something like that. The kind of thing where you sit and write and plan the poem, that's impossible. For me, either the idea arises or it doesn't. It can be a big limitation, but it's no one's fault. We are what we are. It's a type. There's nothing to do.

What relationship do you have with language? Anyone who writes poetry has a very specific relationship with language. In your case, we have the impression of a distance. In the same way that you write "one impossible step from God," language seems to be one impossible step from reality.

Yes. If I were talking about being and the ineffable, it wouldn't work. It's generally said that what cannot be said must be silent. But it's the opposite: what cannot be said becomes a symbol, it becomes a metaphor, it becomes poetry, it becomes blah-blah-blah the size of a train, it becomes ideology, etc., etc. Dealing with what can't be said, you just have to go all in. But you end up getting tired of it, too.

You like to play with words. Maybe that's where one can find some of the humor in your texts. In the poem "Series," for example, you play with the words "lucid" and "ludic."

Poets sometimes go for the word, draw out the word, sometimes we go for assonance, but it happens that we have rationality and assonance at the same time. Poetry is a game with language itself. It's a ludic thing. Maybe it's lucid too, I don't know. A game that comes up with something, a result, who knows what. You're right, it's more or less like that. After all, art is a serious game. Basically, it's a joke, but it's a serious joke. All of culture seems to be a serious game, doesn't it? It's both, time and eternity.

Seriousness, gravity and lightness, all at once. Because it's too serious, for God's sake. Gravity, gravidity, enough! Weight . . . there's a lot of weight in real life.

[. . .]

What does "attentive to the real" mean?

I don't know, I just think it's right. That's all I can say about it.

JOTABÊ MEDEIROS

The poet Orides Fontela is homeless. On the verge of eviction, she took shelter earlier in the week in a student dormitory on Avenida São João, where a loyal friend offered her a sofa to sleep on.

In reality, Orides never had a place in the world. She doesn't know about her relatives ("Maybe a cousin and an uncle, who neither help nor hinder"); she keeps no photos of past loves. Her existence is delineated by the poetry that has made her, according to people like Antonio Candido, Davi Arriguci and Marilena Chauí, one of the most important contemporary Brazilian poets.

Graduated in Philosophy from USP, she has read Heidegger and structuralists, but prefers poets like Baudelaire, Mallarmé, Wallace Stevens. Her book Web has just been published. The City of São Paulo purchased 1,065 copies for the Salas de Leitura program for high school students.

From her temporary couch, she granted this interview.

You are considered to be one of the most important Brazilian poets . . .

I don't have an instrument to measure poets. The critics are saying this, it's their task to examine.

Do you consider yourself influenced by someone?

Of course. Brazilian symbolists, such as Alphonsus de Guimaraens, then the moderns, Bandeira, João Cabral. All these interesting Brazilians. But there comes a time when you find your own way of writing and nothing influences you anymore.

Do you live on poetry?

I live on a pension. Since I retired from my job as a pre-primary teacher, I've received 423.00 reais a month.

[. . .]

Which poets and intellectuals do you spend time with today?

None. I used to show my poems to some critics from São Paulo, but today they think I've made my work more accessible, that I've become popular. They're no longer interested in reading what I write. I found out how alone I am on the night of *Web*'s release, in a bar on Alameda Franca Street. It was great, really nice, but it wasn't literary, it was legal. There were only lawyers there. They all came because of my friend Silvio Rodrigues. There wasn't a single critic, a single poet.

Is there anything you can do about it?

Nothing. They think I've become too accessible, that I've lowered myself, so they scorn me. But being simple and straightforward is much harder than being baroque. To be baroque, all you need is a little book culture. To be simple, you have to be a poet.

from THE REVERSE OF THE VERSE

MARILENE FELINTO

Do you have problems being with people?

Sometimes they call me quarrelsome. I don't know how to get along very well. First, I'm an only child. I was raised very shy, closed in. Second, I have to live in a middle-class environment, in which I wasn't raised. My manners are a little coarse. I didn't drink tea as a child, as they say. Even though I drink it now, it doesn't do any good. And sometimes I can shock people. Especially when I tell the truth. I have to learn to put on a little mask. Sometimes I feel a little insignificant among a lot of middle-class people, fellow poets who are well-off. That's what makes me aggressive with them.

Do you have friends today?

My circle of relationships is very small. One of the things I thought I could achieve with poetry was to have more friends. I'm not getting them. I can get fame from poetry, but I can't change my class background. I was born a proletarian and I still am. This class separation gives me the biggest problem.

How does the difference in social class hinder your relationships?

It's our type of background, the way they look at us . . . When I think someone is looking down on me, I attack. I've gotten better. I had the idea that I was more or less an eccentric personality. They were letting me in because I wrote good poetry, but it seemed like I was being treated as a curiosity. I'm getting over it.

[. . .]

Do you regret not having a profession that allowed you to earn more money?

I'm not the kind of person who wants to put things together. That's not what I want. If I had attended a college that gave me a more reasonable profession, I would have studied pedagogy, to be a school principal. A civil servant's career is like a horse's tail, it grows down.

AFTERWORD

RICARDO DOMENECK

ORIDES DE LOURDES TEIXEIRA FONTELA was born on
April 21, 1940 in São João da Boa Vista, a small city in São
Paulo State famous for the brightness of its light and its spec-
tacular sunsets. Her father was an illiterate planer operator and
carpenter/cabinetmaker ("he could write his name and knew
numbers"). Her mother tended house; semi-literate, she taught
her daughter to read and write with "slaps and ear-pulling." At
an early age, Orides Fontela began reciting poems in church
and school. Her poetry was discovered in a newspaper by an old
schoolmate, the critic Davi Arrigucci Jr., who championed her
work and helped her edit and publish her first book. The critic
Antonio Candido helped arrange for her higher education at
the University of São Paulo. She was licensed in Philosophy in
1972, taught primary school for a time, and was a librarian until
her early retirement. She was an early Brazilian Zen initiate,
perhaps the first woman, but left the monastery because her
mind was "too chaotic."

In her lifetime, she published around 300 poems spread over
five books. Her third book of poems, *Alba*, won the Prémio
Jabuti, one of Brazil's most prestigious literary awards.

At times a difficult person, she was avowedly uninterested
in sex, or romantic relationships. She had few friends in the

literary world; the literary friendships she did have were often tumultuous. She never married. In every interview Fontela gave, there are always questions about her being unmarried and resolutely single, as if her private life were just as important, just as interesting as her poetry. She grew very weary of such questions.

In the months before her death, she was evicted from her apartment, and was a guest on talk shows, where she publicly asked for a job. She was alternately gossiped about and acknowledged as one of the great Brazilian poets. She died of tuberculosis exacerbated by alcoholism and poverty on November 2, 1998 and was saved from a pauper's grave by the actions of her few friends.

Her importance was was acknowledged when *Collected Poetry* was published by Cosac Naify (Poesia Reunida, 1969-1996, Rio de Janeiro, 2006). *Complete Poetry* (*Poesia Completa*, Hedra, São Paulo 2015), adds 20-odd previously unpublished poems written near the end of her life. *Orides the Riddle* (*O enigma Orides*), a novelistic biography by Gustavo de Castro, was published by Hedra in 2015. In 2019, Moinhos (Belo Horizonte) published *Orides Fontela—Every Word Is Cruelty* (*Orides Fontela—Toda Palavra É Crueldade*), a collection of her prose and interviews.

· · ·

It is customary to describe Orides Fontela's *temperament* in biographical notes, and then immediately to discard biography in favor of descriptions of her "lean," "concise," "crystalline" poetry. These adjectives make sense in a description of the poet's work: in her poems the first-person singular seems to be

114

consistently exiled from the verbs.[14] Orides Fontela's biography may not matter that much in a formal evaluation of her work, but there is at least one way of thinking about the connection between the work and the poet's life. In the case of Fontela, would not her physical and material poverty be linked to her stylistic stripping-down, the very paucity of her poetry? A person who owned no property, who felt neither the need nor the desire for a love relationship, perhaps Fontela was uninterested in praising anything but oxygen. Perhaps her poverty led her to abandon adornment and poetic beautification:

THE TRADES

Fruit for
     acid
sun for
     secret
ocean for
     nucleus

space for
     escape
escape for
     silence

—wealth for
     nakedness.

---

14. See Translator's Afterword.

Her poetry is often described as "neo-symbolist." ("Neo-symbolist, my granny," she once said in an interview.) Her use of simple nouns—"bird," "mirror," "river" for example—invite us to see them as "symbols." But something very important separates the work of Orides Fontela from the Brazilian neo-symbolist poets, of whom today we only read Cecília Meireles and Henriqueta Lisboa.[15] In her best poems, Orides Fontela demonstrates the linguistic attention of a post-war poet living a historical moment that demanded, in the use of symbols, an awareness of their being signs. She knew to nourish her symbology by filtering it through language. Read, for example, the poem "Swan" from the book *Alba* (1983):

SWAN

To humanize the swan
is to violate it. But
then who will tell us
the peevish splendor
— the presence of swan?

How say it? Dense
word wounds
white
expels presence and—human—
is splendor memory
and blood.

---

15. To my knowledge, Orides Fontela never mentioned Cecília Meireles or Henriqueta Lisboa as influences; however, she must have been aware of their work, to some extent.

116

And

remains

not swan: the

word

—the word itself

swan.

In Orides Fontela, nouns ebb and flow between symbol and sign, as if poetic language, in its multiple capacity for concretion and abstraction, moved tidally. If Fontela is linked by temperament to poets like Cecília Meireles and, in turn, to Cruz e Sousa,[16] her "signic" symbolism makes Orides Fontela closer, I believe, to Henriqueta Lisboa, a poet we ought to be reading again; not the early Henriqueta Lisboa, but the poet conscious of the games and devices of language and symbols/signs. I am speaking of the poet Henriqueta Lisboa becomes from the 1950s on, especially in books like *Além da Imagem or Reverberações* (1976). For example, these two poems from *Reverberações*:

CALENDAR

Hushed and fictive

flowering falls

---

16. João da Cruz e Sousa was one of the truly great Brazilian symbolist poets. A Wikipedia article gives the basic facts. It is worth noting that for decades, Brazilian critics and literary historians passed over the Brazilian symbolist movement in favor of Brazilian Parnassianism. The few acceptable symbolist poets (Cruz e Sousa was not one of them) were called "pre-modernist," and the rest were elided or even devalued. It seems to me that the concept of "pre-modernism" no longer holds as much sway, and that a greater respect is now given to Brazilian symbolism. This is all to the good.

from the tree
of days.

RETINUE

Follow the king
everywhere
before his crown
falls off.

Such "signic" symbolism also brings Orides Fontela close to a poet like Wallace Stevens, who made the appropriation of the world by consciousness, via language, the poetic game par excellence. But, if in Stevens this clash and organization of the world by consciousness is a human and only human subject, without a shadow of transcendence, Orides Fontela wove a mystical thread into her poetry. Her books move rotationally, undergoing a scouring, and then settling in concretion on the ground of the world, in the one-page poem, only to immediately abandon themselves to an ethereal, symbolically laden environment in the poem on the very next page.

It is as if the poetry of Orides Fontela was unable definitively to decide between the destruction of the world by a centripetal, or by a centrifugal force. As I see it, her poems possess, despite their polished, glassy surface, a violence with few parallels in Brazilian post-war poetry. The same torment may perhaps be sensed in Hilda Hilst's prose and poetry, but for this other avowed mystic the solution was the scornful exuberance of the flood. Orides Fontela, who never owned anything, preferred the desert. Something of this ebb and flow, between the concrete and the abstract, between the symbol and the sign, can be seen in several poems. In "Saint Sebastian," from the book *Helianthus* (1973), we read the centripetal concretization of the symbol becoming a sign, the word becoming flesh, the myth gaining a body of blood and bone:

SAINT SEBASTIAN

Arrows
—cruel—in the body

arrows
in fresh blood

arrows
in naked youth

arrows
—firm—confirm
   the flesh.

The first time I read this poem, I was standing outside the library of the Faculty of Letters at the University of São Paulo, and I felt a little dizzy. The title invites us to expect the ethereality of a hagiography. Nothing could seem further from a poetics of the corporeal and the physical. The first images give us the statue of the saint, the myth. We imagine this non-existent being, we think of the mystical, of unthinkable sacrifice.

However, Orides Fontela's slow progression is that of a snake boat, as it takes us to the last verse, when what is revealed is not the statue of the saint, but the living flesh of a man before sainthood. The poem seems to me to be almost brutally violent. Sebastian stops being myth and metaphor and becomes a figure, a figure as a concept of Christian theology, A FIGURE, in which a historical event is linked to and prefigures another historical event, two distinct and temporally segregated facts foreseeing a final event that reveals its meanings. Here, Orides Fontela's poetics is revealed in all her belief in the historicity of her work.

In "Clime," also from *Alba* (1983), such a two-way street of language is strongly present—centrifugal abstraction, centripetal concretion, sign, symbol: language.

CLIME

At this marked spot: field where
a single tree
rises

and the elongated
gesture
absorbing
all the silence—ascends and
                              stills

(sound before voice
pre-living

or beyond voice
and life)

at this marked spot: still
                              field
secret   lust   schism
being
celebrates

— mute elastic
  elliptic
  eucalyptus.

It is in this book, *Alba*, that I believe Orides Fontela found her
angle of repose. The book is a bright spot in the 1980s. Con-
temporary poet, postwar poet, Orides Fontela knew how to
write poetry with symbols inherited from an ancient tradition,
but informed by a world in which Saussure, Wittgenstein, and
Jakobson had written. Orides Fontela knew that silence did not
come from a lack of answers, but from our inability and lim-
itation when asking questions through language, whose limits,
according to Wittgenstein, are the limits of our world.

SPHINX

There are no questions.
Obdurate silence grows wild.

It is tempting to mythologize this woman, who lived as she
lived and wrote these poems like cubes of concentrated energy,

waiting to explode in the reader's eye. Her poems, at first sight so simple, demand concentration and attention from those able to whisper, as in the exordial poem from *Alba*:

> One step
> from the bird
> I breathe
> in.

Yes, maddening lucidity. Orides Fontela died in a public hospital in 1998, without a close family, destitute as a poet, exactly one hundred years after the death of Cruz e Sousa and the transport of his body by cattle car to Rio de Janeiro. For me, these two dates, 1898 and 1998, open and close twentieth century Brazilian poetry.

TRANSLATOR'S NOTE

CHRIS DANIELS

Words are gossamer in the world of granite.
KIM STANLEY ROBINSON

When I first read Orides Fontela's poems, several of them reminded me very strongly of the iconography of certain ecstatic poets: the eyebrow, the curl of hair upon the forehead, the mole on the cheek of the beloved. She was surely a mystic, to some extent, although she denied it. (The reader will notice that she contradicted herself, or seemed to.) In no way am I a mystic. I am not in the least a metaphysical sort of person. Fontela had a degree in Philosophy; I dropped out of high school. At the very least, she believed in a cosmic organizing principle, which she called Love or God. I am godless. However, I am happy to know that I am a human among humans. The words "we" and "us" occur quite often in this book. Solidarity exists here. Ultimately, this is what I get from the poetry of Orides Fontela.

Fontela organized her books very carefully. Each begins with a poem about writing and ends with a poem about silence. (Perhaps she knew, or intuited, that the universe and everything in it consists mostly of empty space). I have tried wherever possible to mirror her practice. While this selection contains less than a third of her output, I hope that I have been able to give readers an idea of her concerns, her technique, and the variety of her work. I have moved poems around freely, but the ordering of poems is close to the order in which they appear in the originals.

Orides Fontela resisted all labels, all attempts to situate her work in a particular movement, school, tendency, or tradition. While her bird and flower, water and stone, blood and star can surely be seen as symbols (I find it very difficult not to see them as such, and I am hardly alone in that), they are also concrete entities and objects, instances of the immensely variegated matter of which we are made and which exists throughout the universe. If symbols, perhaps they are symbolic only of themselves, or only of themselves as signs and symbols (can that even make sense?). Perhaps they are hypostatic, despite Fontela's own statement in an interview that she was no Platonist. I do not know, and feel no need to know.

The interviews have been severely edited, as they contain much material already covered in the two (of three) brief texts she wrote about her work. All the footnotes in this book were added by me.

> Who speaks in the poems of Orides Fontela? [This question] calls attention to her preference for infinitives, abstract nouns, and substantives referring to inanimate or in some way unusual elements, as agents of verbal action. This preference is so evident that one sometimes thinks that the number of poems that contain a first-person singular or plural subjective verb must be smaller than it is.
>
> — FLORA SÜSSEKIND[17]

17. Flora Süssekind, "Seis poetas e alguns comentários," *Revista USP* no. 2 (August 30, 1989): 175–92.

Orides Fontela almost never wrote the word "eu," the subjective form of the Portuguese first-person singular pronoun. Romance Languages are inflected. The conjugation of verbs makes pronouns to some extent extraneous. The omission of subjective pronouns causes no confusion.[18] Indeed, poets do very often omit pronouns for the sake of concision, music, scansion, and so forth. However, in her three hundred or so poems, I find only three instances of "eu." In comparison, in the complete poetry of Ana Cristina Cesar, an important poet roughly contemporary with Fontela, "eu" occurs about four hundred times.

In this translation, all but three instances of the word "I" are the result of the translation of a verb in the first-person singular without a pronoun. The exceptions occur in "Settling" and "Rose" in *Transposition*. An attempt to account for her practice would make this a book full of imperatives. Apart from the instances in the two poems mentioned above, I view every appearance of the word "I" as the result of an insoluble conundrum. My hope is for readers to think of the word "I" as silent.

To this conundrum, I would add another question, from what place does Orides Fontela speak in her poems? According to John Howard,

> She lived in a tiny [apartment] not far from the downtown Boca do Crime ("mouth of crime"), the city's oldest red-light district, a noisy, polluted, unsightly, overbuilt decadence. Where was the nearest tree, bird? What [was] the source of

---

18. There are exceptions. For example, the first-person present of the verb *motivar* (to motivate, to bring about, to base, to ground) could, in some cases, conceivably be confused for the noun *motivo* (reason, cause, motif, motive).

her favorite words: silence, white, pure, water and sea, star and space?[19]

I cannot answer Howard's questions, but we know that Fontela rejected confessionalism. We know she was interested in Christian mysticism and Zen Buddhism. We know she lived as an ascetic, by choice or by circumstance. I feel that she wished to express ideas, to write about the world, the universe, and *perception itself*, while taking her person out of the picture, however impossible that may be.

In places, I took great liberties, but have tried to reproduce as closely as possible the punctuation, unhyphenated line breaks, and turns of syntax wherever and whenever they occur in the poems. For example, Fontela's use of gerunds and gerundives tell me that there is always something happening, always something about to happen in the universe.

While I am acutely aware that most Anglophone readers will have little or no knowledge of Lusophone literature, and therefore Orides Fontela's importance in the literature of her country, I hope that this book will inspire some readers to learn Portuguese and begin to familiarize themselves with an eight-hundred-year-old poetic tradition.

My most childish dream is to be translated. It's completely silly, of course. But it must be nice to be international.

—ORIDES FONTELA

Oakland, October 2021

19. John Howard, Orides Fontela: A Sketch, *Brazzil Magazine*, 2/1/2002. Online only.

ACKNOWLEDGMENTS

About 25 years ago, Dana Stevens loaned me her copy of *Rosá-cea* (*Rosace*) (the translation of "Impressions" is mostly hers). Later on, Rodrigo Garcia Lopes gifted me with his copy of *Trevo* (*Clover*), the collected poems published in the late 80s. Virna Teixeira sent me *Teia* (*Web*) and answered many questions. Virna cleared the way. Rodrigo read an early version of the full translation. He and Virna saved me from more than a few howling blunders. I would never have been able to continue, let alone finish, without them, and I am deeply grateful. John Howard's translation of *Alba* was a great help, and I strongly urge people to read that translation and Howard's sympathetic reminiscence "Orides Fontela: A Sketch" in *Brazzil Magazine*, which is still available online.

I will always be grateful and beholden to my dear friends and comrades Chris Chen, John Gould, Sidney Maxwell and Susan Maxwell. Chris helped me with the initial editing of this book; he, John, Sidney and Susan help me to continue being the person I have become.

It would be impossible to be more thankful to the artists Kim Bennett and Amelia Konow, whose beautiful works have occasionally responded to Orides Fontela with so much enthusiasm, love, and respect. I feel very lucky to know these two very talented, sensitive artists. I need to mention my dear Anja Weiser Flower, who is one of the most intelligent people I know. I have learned so much about art from her; her political acuity and generous nature are crucial in my life. The three of them have had a profound effect on these translations. Knowing them has been and will continue to be an immensely pleasurable—and delightfully humbling—learning experience. Their examples live in me.

Josely Vianna Baptista helped me acquire translations rights and helped me compose business letters. Rafael Mantovani helped with others. I have no experience writing formal Portuguese letters. I am very grateful.

In my opinion, Ricardo Domeneck is one of the truest poets currently writing in any language, anywhere in the world. His afterword has helped me immensely. I cannot thank him enough.

I owe a vast and special gratitude to everybody at Nightboat, and I am grateful to the late Maria Helena Teixeira de Oliveira, Fontela's literary executor.

To all those who have read earlier versions of the translated poems; to all those who have said lovely things to me after readings: your encouragement kept me going for the 25 years it's taken. You know who you are, but I have to mention the late, much-missed Ben Hollander. I am so proud to have been his friend.

I dedicate these translations in gratitude to the memory of Orides Fontela's cousin, Maria Helena Teixeira de Oliveira; to Fontela's relatives; and to the memory of my family: David, Rita, and Sally, whom I miss every day.

Oakland, March 2023

BIBLIOGRAPHY

POETRY

Poesia Reunida 1969-1996 (Cosac Naify, Rio de Janeiro, 2006).
Poesia Completa (Hedra, São Paulo, 2015).

PROSE

"Sobre poesia e filosofia—um depoimento," In *Poesia (e) Filosofia: por poetas-filósofos em atuação no Brasil*, ed. Alberto Pucheu (Belo Horizonte, Editora Moinhos, 2018).
"Nas trilhas do *Trevo*," in *Artes e ofícios da poesia*, ed. Augusto Massi (Porto Alegre, Artes e Ofício Editora, 1991), 259.
Orides Fontela—toda palavra é crueldade (ed. Nathan Matos, Belo Horizonte, Moinhos, 2019).

INTERVIEWS

Entrevista do Mês. Orides Fontela, "Poesia, sexo, destino," interview by Augusto Massi, José Maria Cançado, and Flávio Quintiliano. *Leia livros*, January 23, 1989.
"Uma conversa com Orides Fontela," interview by Michel Riaudel, *Cahiers du CREPAL*, no. 5 (1998): 147-177.

"Orides Fontela combate despejo com sua poesia," interview by Jotabê Medeiros, *Estadão*, April 12, 1996.

"O avesso do verso," interview by Marilene Felinto, *Revista Marie Claire*, September 1996.

AFTERWORD

Orides Fontela (1940-1998), by Ricardo Domeneck. Originally published on the *Modo de Usar & Co.* blog on April 15, 2008. Used with author's permission.

ORIDES FONTELA was born in 1940 in São João da Boa Vista, in the interior of São Paulo, and died in 1998. She studied philosophy at the Universidade de São Paulo (USP). In 1969 her first book, *Transposição*, was published, followed by four more collections. Her third collection, *Alba* (1983), won the Jabuti Prize, one of the most important prizes in Brazil. In France, a large selection of her poems appeared in translation under the title *Trèfle* (2000). In 2006 the Brazilian publishing house Cosac Naify published her collected poems, *Poesia Reunida*.

RICARDO DOMENECK (Brazil, 1977) is a poet, performer and producer. He has published nine collections of poetry and two collections of prose in Brazil. His work has been translated and published in Germany, Spain, and the Netherlands. He has collaborated with Brazilian and German musicians such as Tetine, Lea Porcelain, Nelson Bell, and Francisco Bley. He lives and works in Berlin, Germany.

CHRIS DANIELS (New York City, 1956) is a prolific, widely published, self-taught, feral translator of global Lusophone poetry. Recent translations include *a black body* by Lubi Prates (2020) and *The Hammer* by Adelaide Ivánova (2019). He lives in Oakland, California.

NIGHTBOAT BOOKS

Nightboat Books, a nonprofit organization, seeks to develop audiences for writers whose work resists convention and transcends boundaries. We publish books rich with poignancy, intelligence, and risk. Please visit nightboat.org to learn about our titles and how you can support our future publications.

The following individuals have supported the publication of this book. We thank them for their generosity and commitment to the mission of Nightboat Books:

Kazim Ali • Anonymous (8) • Mary Armantrout • Jean C. Ballantyne • Thomas Ballantyne • Bill Bruns • John Cappetta • V. Shannon Clyne • Ulla Dydo Charitable Fund • Photios Giovanis • Amanda Greenberger • Vandana Khanna • Isaac Klausner • Shari Leinwand • Anne Marie Macari • Elizabeth Madans • Martha Melvoin • Caren Motika • Elizabeth Motika • The Leslie Scalapino - O Books Fund • Robin Shanus • Thomas Shardlow • Rebecca Shea • Ira Silverberg • Benjamin Taylor • David Wall • Jerrie Whitfield & Richard Motika • Arden Wohl • Issam Zineh

This book is made possible, in part, by grants from the New York City Department of Cultural Affairs in partnership with the City Council and the New York State Council on the Arts Literature Program.